THE SEA

A visual journey into this wonder

THE COFFEE TABLE BOOKS

ISBN: 9798853043589
Printed in the USA by KIMASAGU STUDIO
Check for more of our books on Amazon

The sea is the interconnected system of all the Earth's oceanic waters,
including the Atlantic, Pacific, Indian, Southern and Arctic Oceans. However,
the word "sea" can also be used for many specific, much smaller bodies of
seawater, such as the North Sea or the Red Sea. The seas have been an
integral element for humans throughout history and culture. Humans
harnessing and studying the seas have been recorded since ancient times,
and evidenced well into prehistory, while its modern scientific study is called
oceanography and maritime space is governed by the law of the sea, with
admiralty law regulating human interactions at sea. The seas provide
substantial supplies of food for humans, mainly fish, but also shellfish,
mammals and seaweed, whether caught by fishermen or farmed underwater.
Other human uses of the seas include trade, travel, mineral extraction, power
generation, warfare, and leisure activities such as swimming, sailing, and
scuba diving. Many of these activities create marine pollution.

The largest terrestrial seas are:
Philippine Sea – 5.695 million km2
Coral Sea – 4.791 million km2
American Mediterranean Sea – 4.200 million km2
Arabian Sea – 3.862 million km2
Sargasso Sea – 3.5 million km2
South China Sea – 3.5 million km2
Weddell Sea – 2.8 million km2
Caribbean Sea – 2.754 million km2
Mediterranean Sea – 2.510 million km2
Gulf of Guinea – 2.35 million km2

In the vast expanse of the world's oceans lies a realm of mystery, power, and untamed beauty. 'The Sea: A visual journey into this wonder' is an exploration into the heart of this elemental force that has captivated humanity since the dawn of time. With each turn of the page, immerse yourself in the rhythmic dance of waves, feel the salty breeze against your skin, and embark on a journey that transcends the boundaries of land and delves into the secrets hidden beneath the surface. From the vibrant coral reefs teeming with life to the deep abyss where darkness reigns, this profound voyage reveals the wonders and intricacies of the sea, unveiling a symphony of life, a testament to the relentless power of nature, and an invitation to embrace the unknown depths that lie within us all.

the sea

Beneath the azure sky's embrace, the sea unfurls its liquid grace, where tides and currents intertwine, revealing nature's grand design.

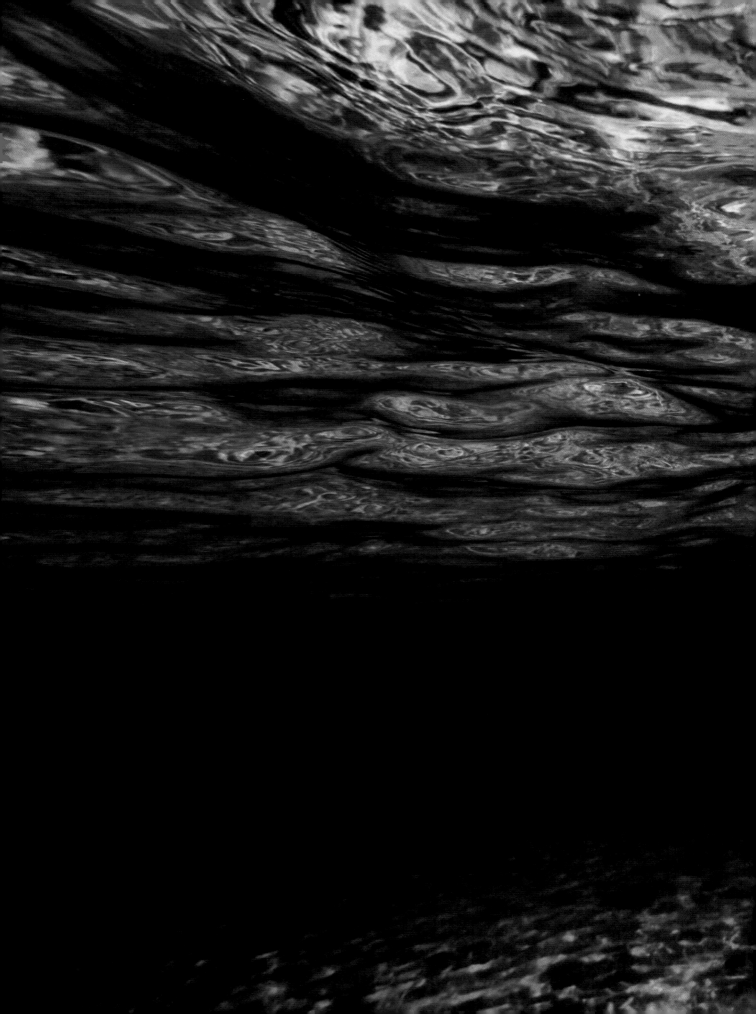

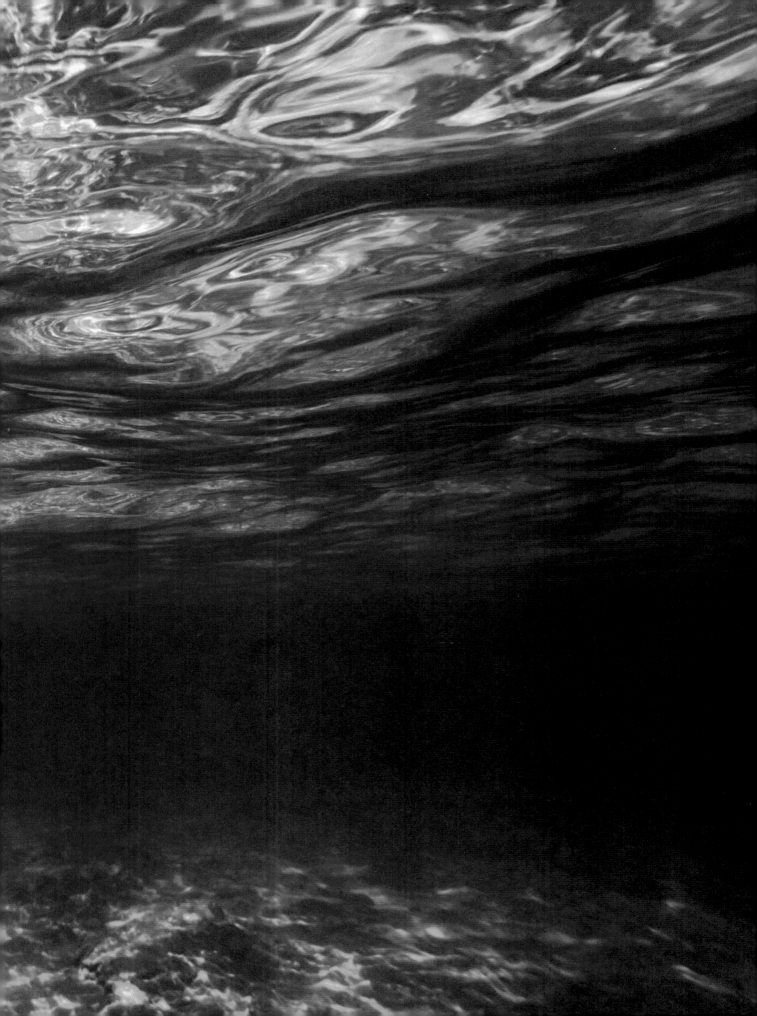

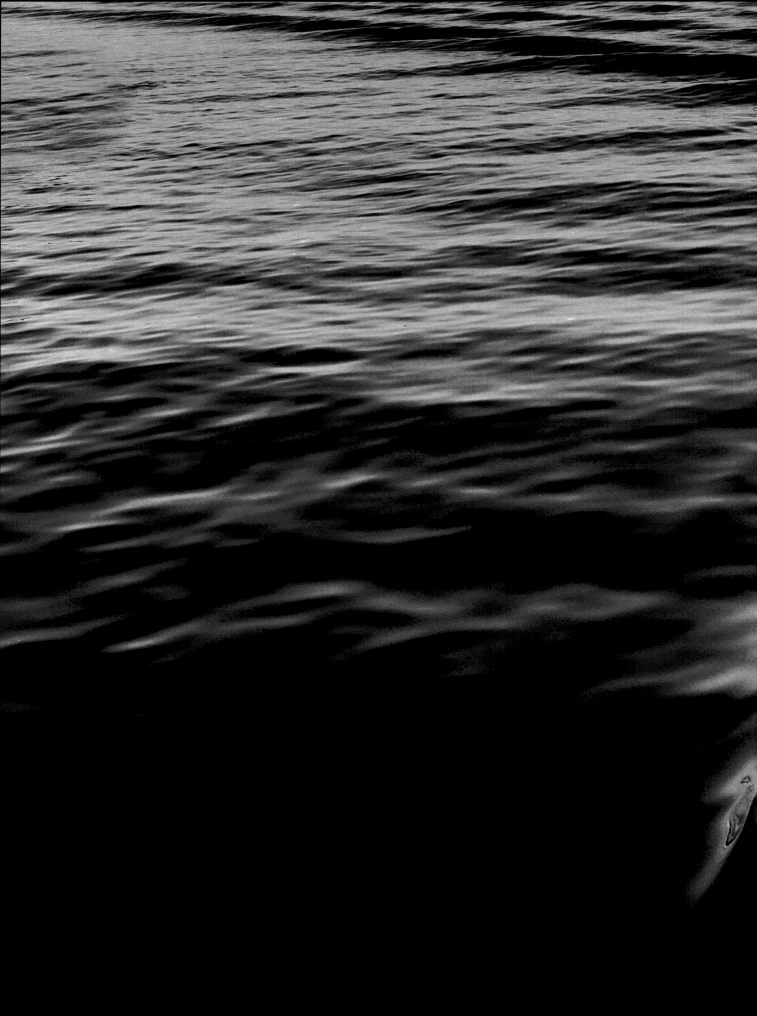

Like a vast mirror,
the sea reflects the
moon's gentle glow,
a celestial ballet
performed below.
Where stars meet the
brine, dreams align.

The sea's rhythm, a soothing song, a symphony where waves belong. Its melodies ebb and flow, a lullaby for hearts that know.

As waves crash upon the shore, they echo tales from distant shores. Each droplet carries whispers old, stories of adventure yet untold.

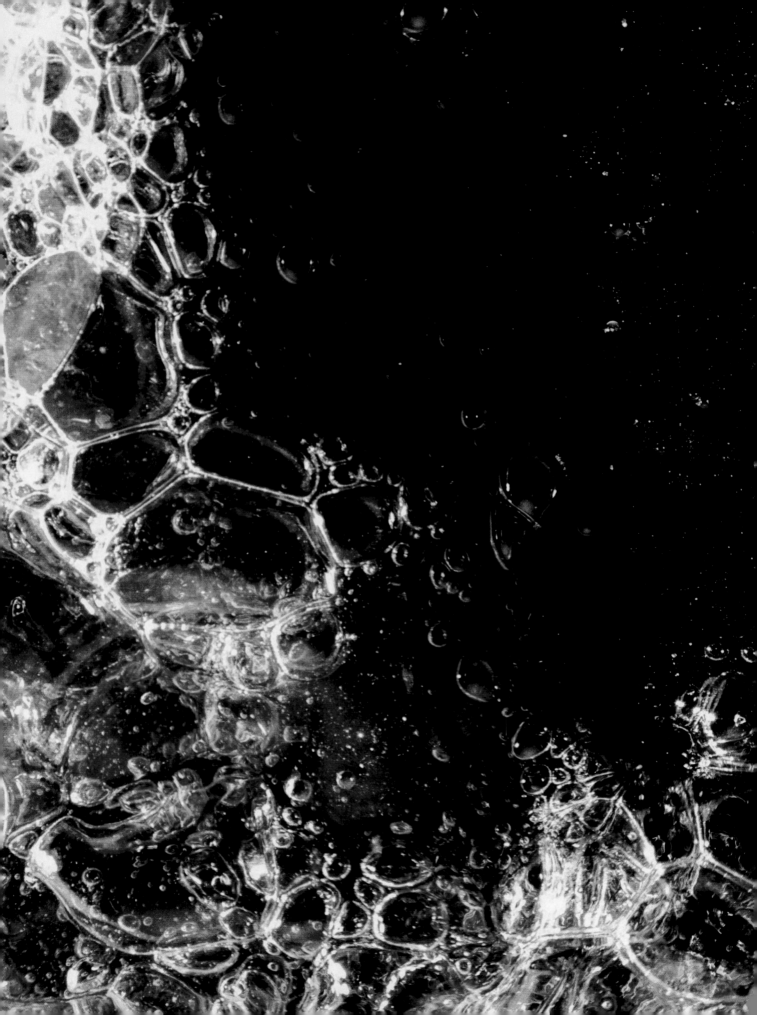

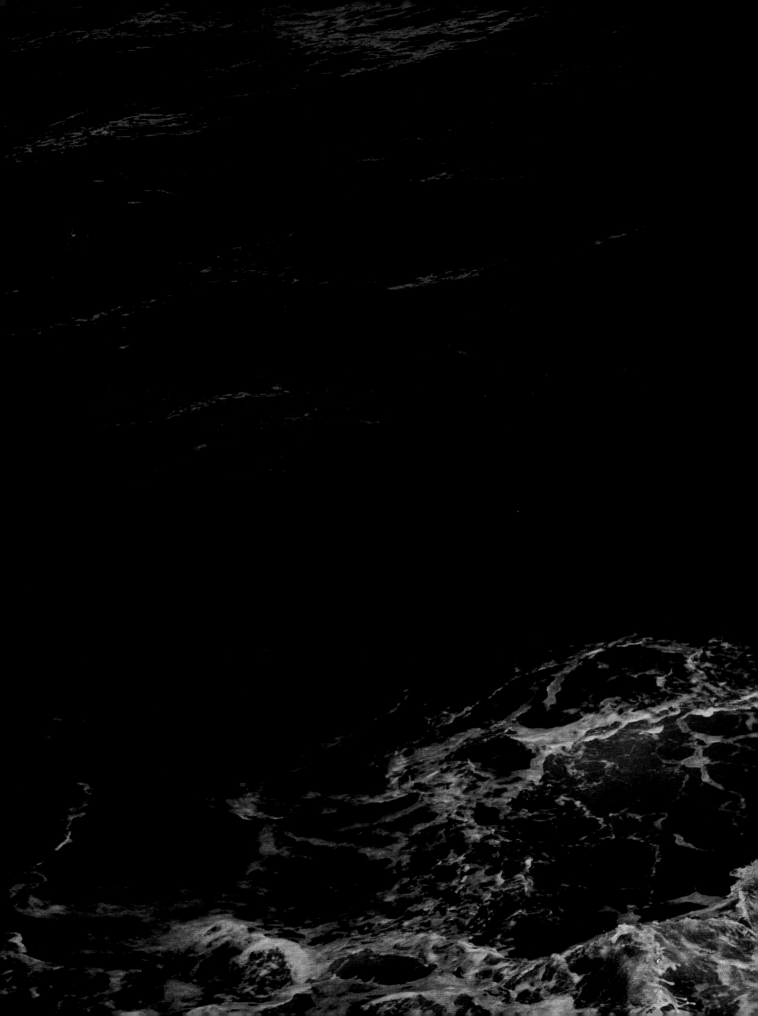

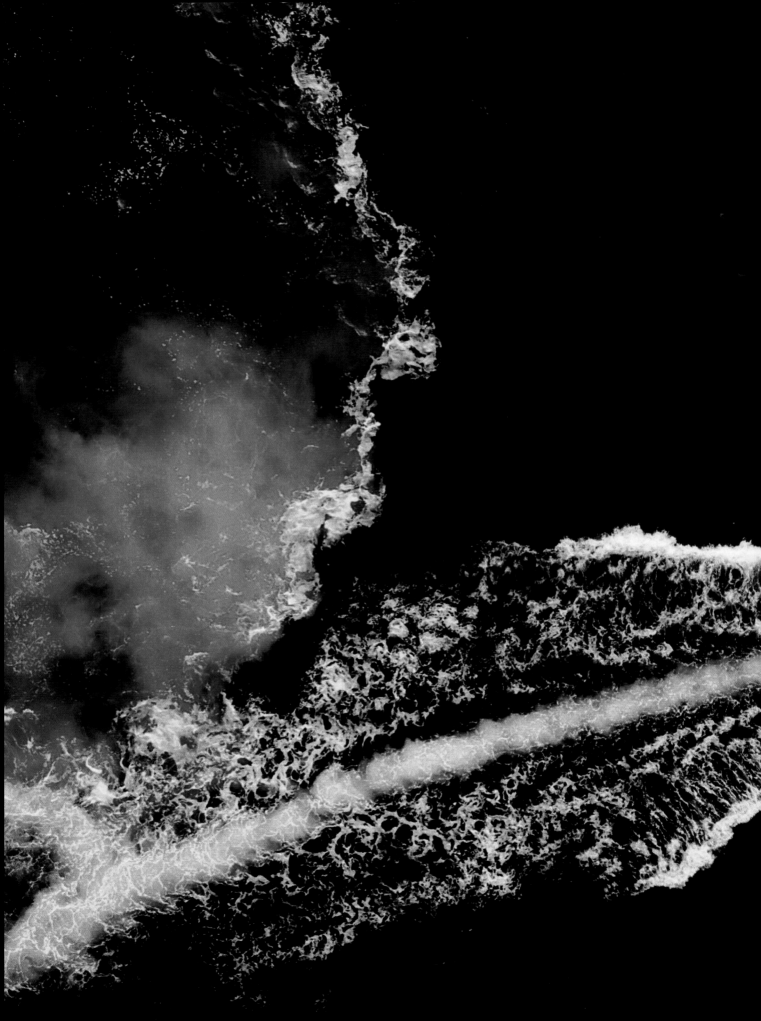

Within the sea's
embrace, treasures
lie in hidden space.
Sunken ships and
ancient lore, secrets
guarded forevermore.

Where land meets
the horizon's gleam,
the sea beckons with
its eternal dream.
A boundless expanse,
a world untamed,
where freedom's
essence is unashamed.

undersea

In the depths where
mysteries lie, the sea
whispers ancient lullabies.
Secrets dance upon its
waves, captivating hearts,
forever enslaved.

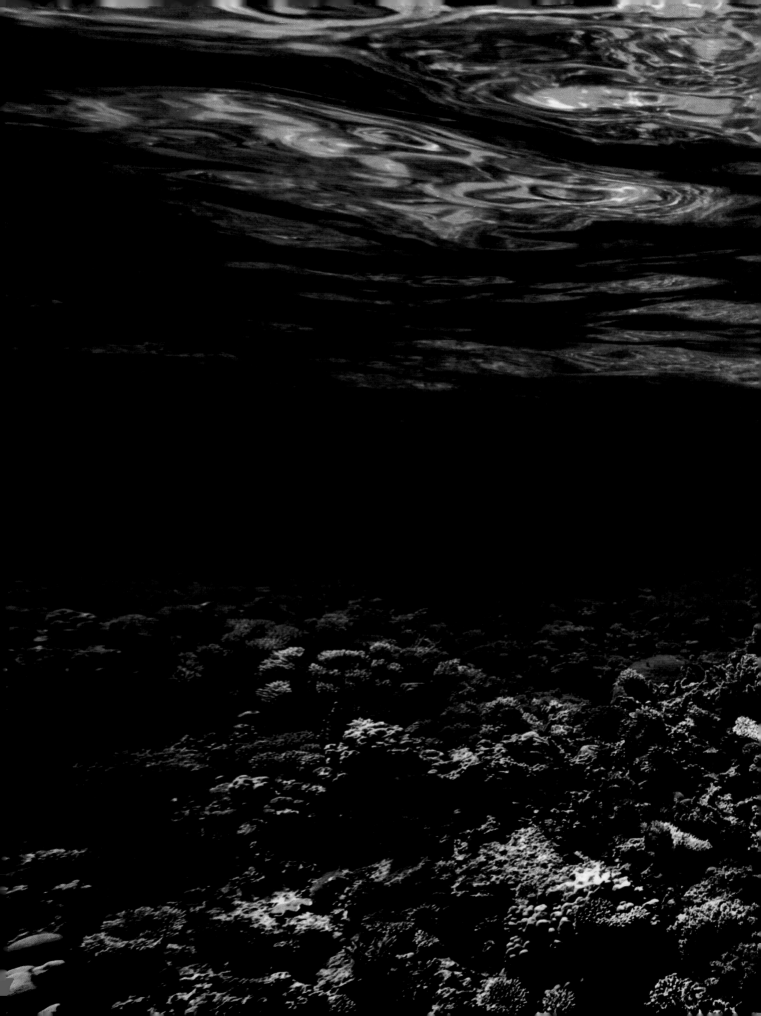

Beneath cerulean
skies, where seagulls
fly, the sea's embrace
invites you to try. Dive
into depths unknown,
where possibilities
are sown.

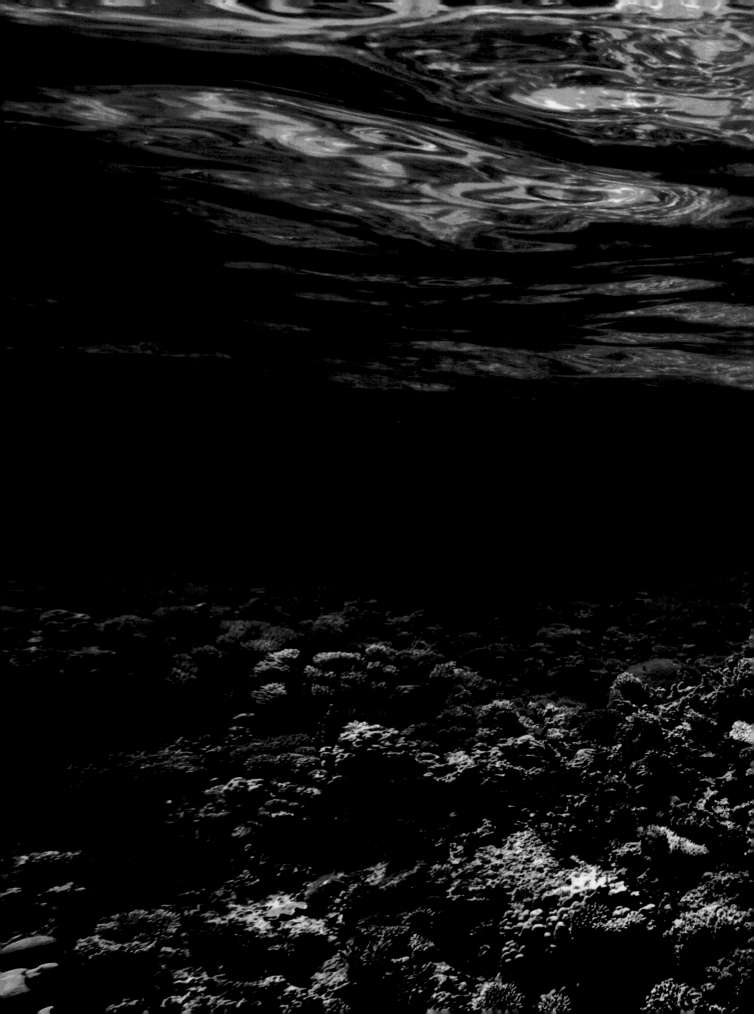

Beneath cerulean
tides, where sunbeams
play, the undersea
realm enchants the
day. Coral castles rise
in hues divine, where
aquatic spirits
gracefully intertwine.

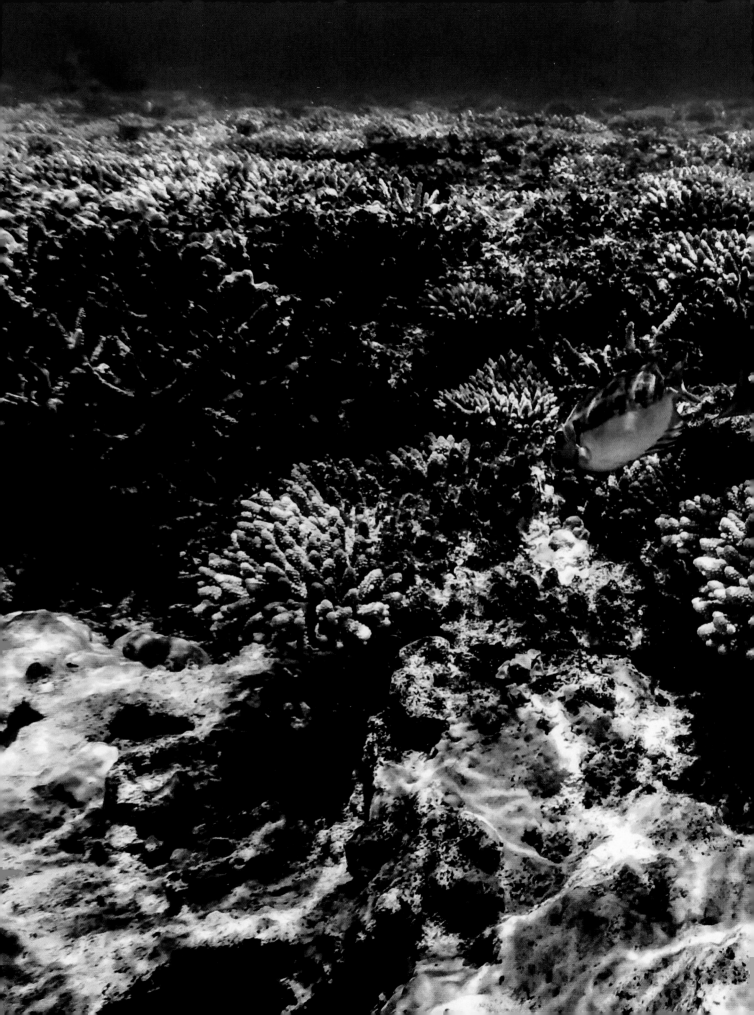

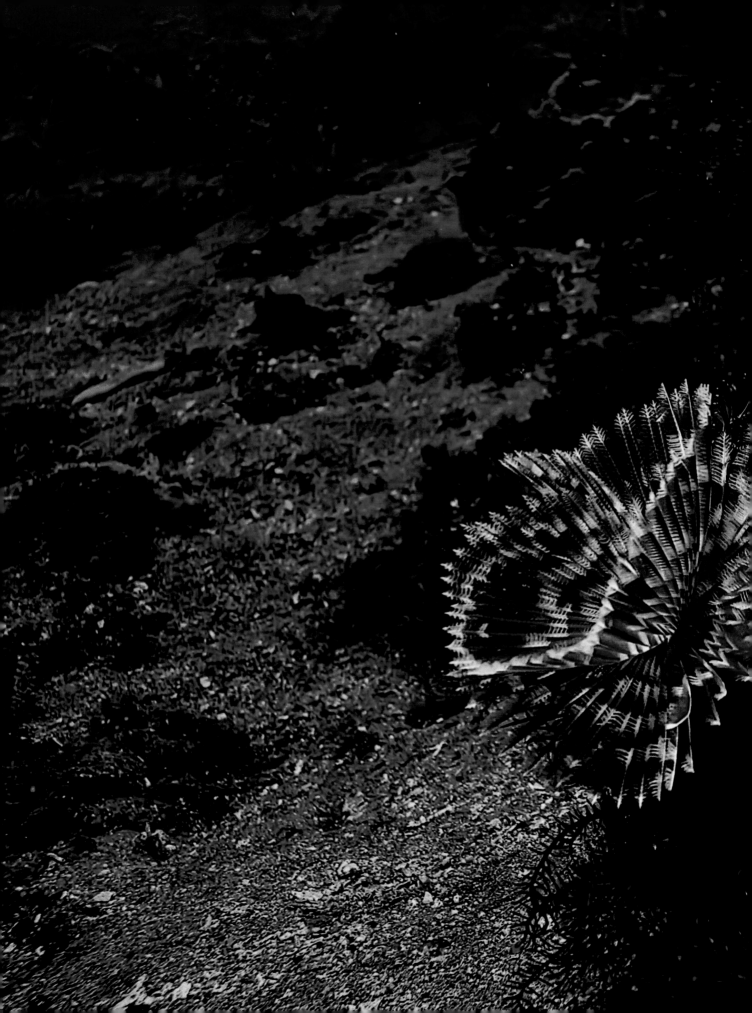

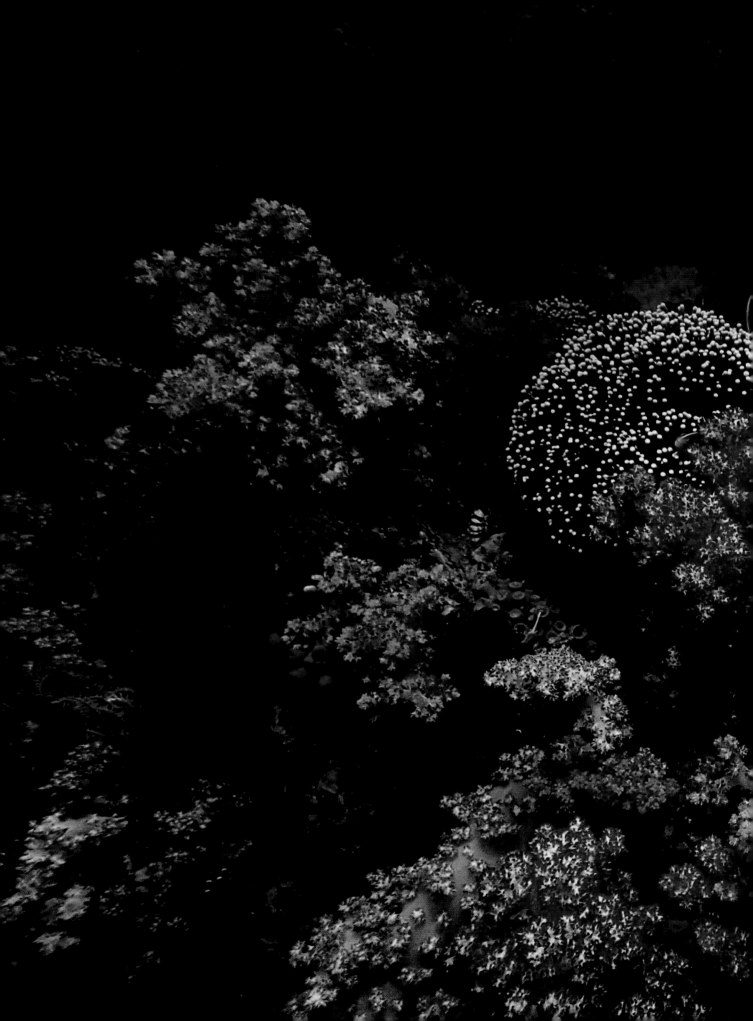

In the depths, a
symphony of blue,
where shadows dance
in mystical hue.
Secrets dwell in
Neptune's keep, where
wonders stir from
the ocean's sleep.

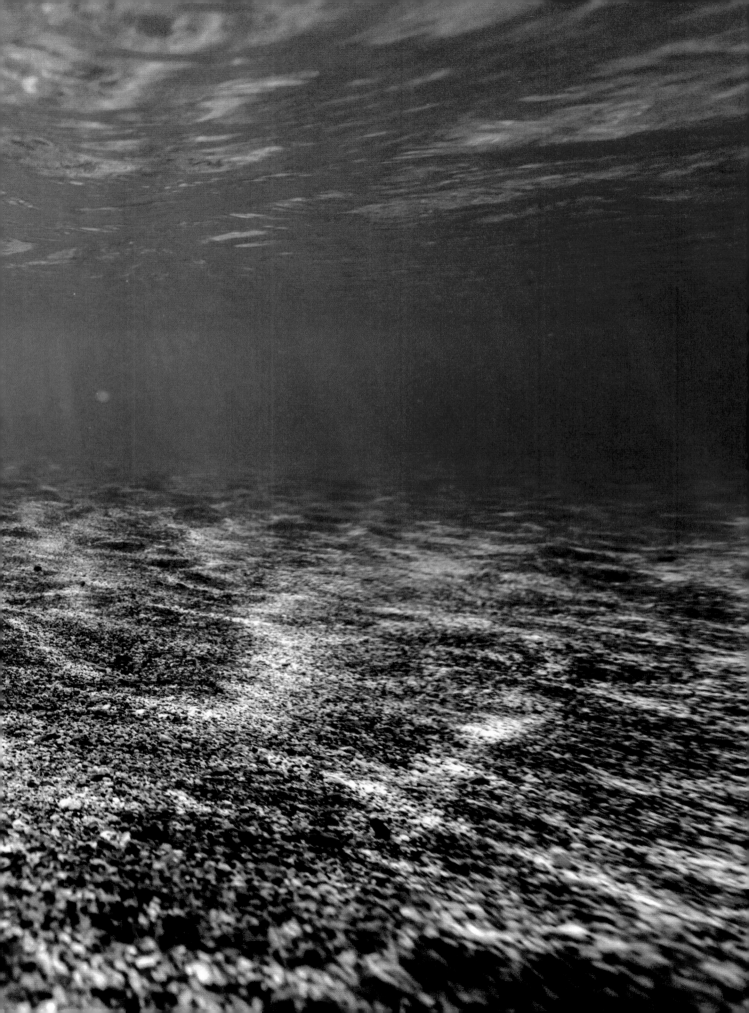

Within the labyrinth of seagrass sway, a cradle of life in a ballet array. Silken whispers weave tales untold, where mermaids dance with pearls of gold.

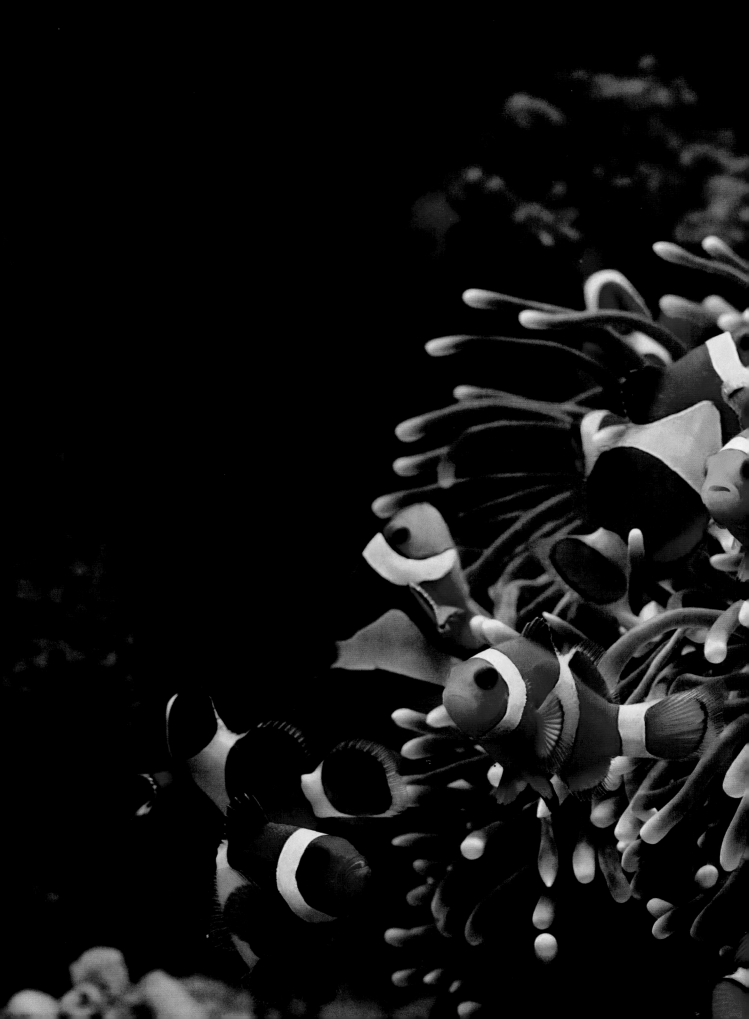

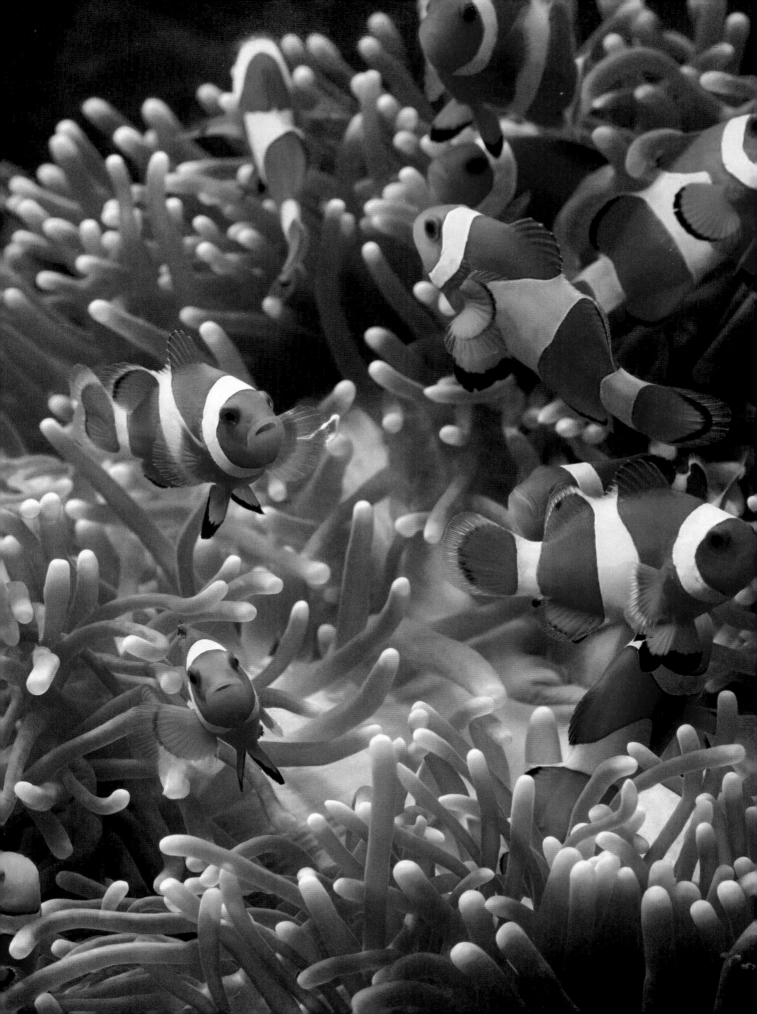

In the depths where
darkness lures,
bioluminescent
wonders endure.
Stars beneath the
waves ignite, painting
a dreamscape in
the night.

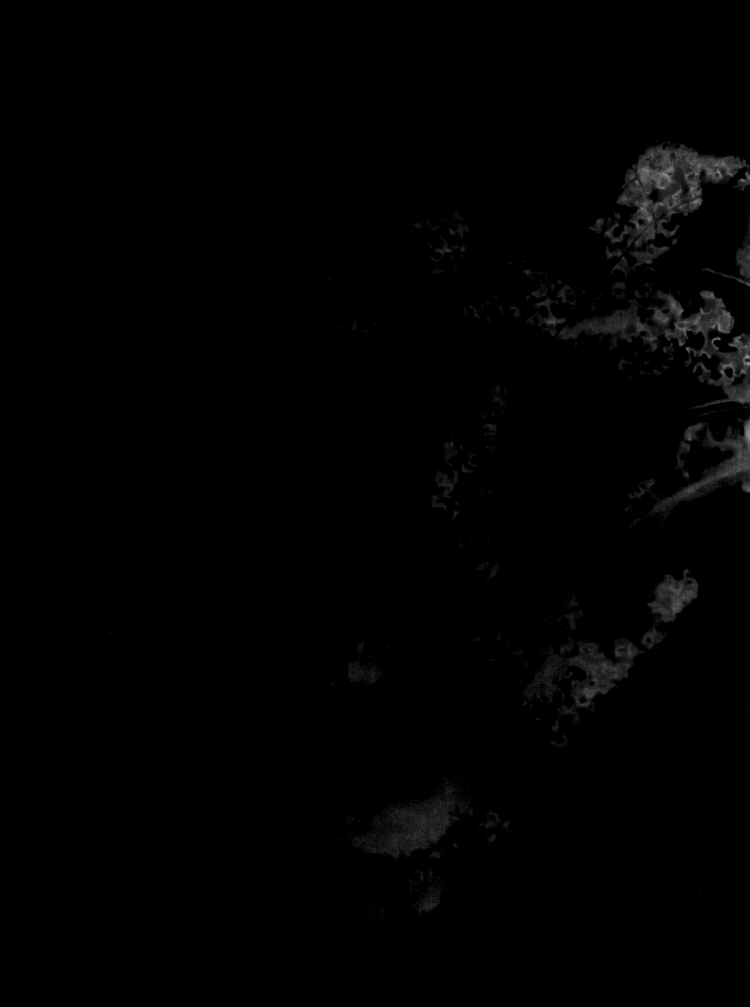

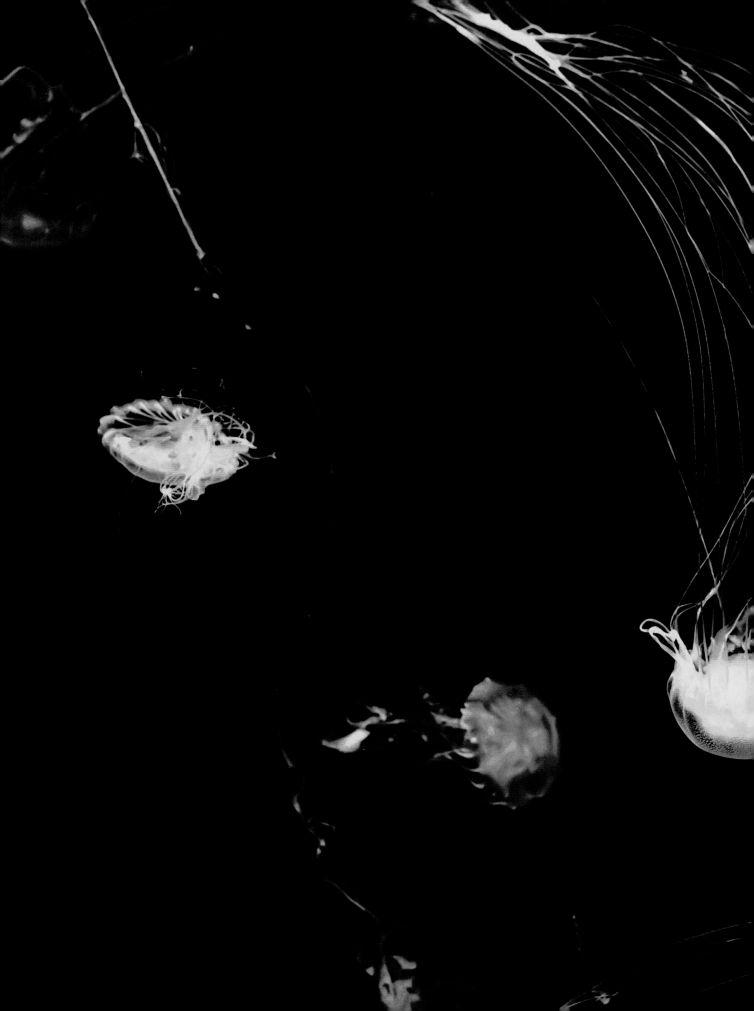